THIS BOOK BELONGS TO:

____

____

Made in the USA
Monee, IL
07 July 2021

73140434R00072